CAJUN&CREOLE COOKING

Designed by Claire Leighton
Recipe photography by Peter Barry
Recipes styled by Bridgeen Deery and Wendy Devenish
Edited by Jillian Stewart
Incidental photography by FPG International

CLB 2809
© 1992 Colour Library Books Ltd, Godalming, Surrey, England.
All rights reserved.
This 1992 edition published by Crescent Books,
distributed by Outlet Book Company Inc., a Random House Company,
40 Engelhard Avenue, Avenel, New Jersey 07001.
Printed and bound in Singapore.
ISBN 0 517 06603 3
8 7 6 5 4 3 2 1

CAJUN & CREOLE COOKING

CRESCENT BOOKS
NEW YORK • AVENEL, NEW JERSEY

INTRODUCTION

Driven from their lands in Canada by the British in the late 18th century, the people from the French colony of Acadia moved south to settle in the fertile bayou country of southern Louisiana. They made a home for themselves in the swampy, mysterious marshland around New Orleans, and a colorful Cajun culture, part French and part American, evolved.

Cajun food was based on French country cooking, but adapted to the local ingredients. Cajun cooks also exchanged ideas with Creole cooks, and some of the Spanish, West Indian and African influence of the latter crept into the Cajun repertoire.

What is Creole cooking? It's American cooking but with a difference. It's Southern cooking, but with further refinement. Its home is New Orleans, where cooking has always been considered an art. This reverence for culinary matters is no doubt traceable to the strong French influence in southern Louisiana. But there were other influences at work on the local cuisine too.

To be considered a Creole in the strictest sense, you would have to be descended from a French or Spanish family who came to the area before 1803. Other groups, including West Indians, had also settled here, all with their individual ideas about what to eat and how to cook it. And it was this amalgamation of different cultures that gave birth to Creole cuisine as we know it today.

Instead of the formality of the food favored by the aristocracy, the French settlers relied mostly on simple country-style dishes, although as the area became more populated grand dining was revived for special occasions. The recipes were altered to suit local ingredients. Rice became a mainstay because it grew easily in the warm, humid climate. Fish and shellfish were abundant, and vegetables such as tomatoes and red and green peppers flourished in the long growing season. The French used herbs to add flavor, the West Indians spices and the Spanish a dash of hot pepper, Africans brought in new vegetables like okra. Thus was born Creole cuisine, definitely Southern and definitely different.

Both Cajun and Creole cooking rely on seafood, rice, herbs, peppers and green onions as staple ingredients, and both are frequently spicy and hot in character. Whatever the similarities or differences, one thing is certain, Cajun and Creole cooking is among the most spirited in America today.

Skyscrapers contrast markedly with the historic and picturesque streets of New Orleans' French Quarter, where the French and Spanish influence on "Creole" architecture is evident.

Gumbo Z'Herbes

Preparation Time: about 25 minutes **Cooking Time:** 2½ hours **Serves:** 6

Gumbo is an African word for okra, which helps to thicken this soup-stew. Z'Herbes refers to all the greens that go into it.

Ingredients

8oz green cabbage leaves
8oz spinach, well washed
1lb spring greens, collard, mustard, beet or turnip greens
4oz chicory (Belgian endive)
1 large bunch watercress, well washed
1 large bunch parsley, well washed
6 carrot and radish tops (if available)
4 cups water
Salt, pepper and a pinch cayenne
2 tbsps butter or margarine
1 large red pepper, seeded and coarsely chopped
Half a bunch green onions, coarsely chopped
8oz okra, trimmed and sliced
1 bay leaf
1 tsp thyme
Pinch cinnamon and nutmeg

Trim any coarse stalks on the cabbage and spinach and wash both well. Wash greens, chicory, watercress, parsley and carrot and radish tops. Bring water to the boil in a large stock pot and add the greens, spinach, cabbage, chicory, watercress, parsley and carrot and radish tops. Return the mixture to the boil, reduce the heat and simmer, partially covered, for about 2 hours. Strain and reserve the liquid. Purée the vegetables in a food processor until smooth, and return to the rinsed out pot. Measure the liquid and make up to 3 cups with water, if necessary.

Melt the butter or margarine, cook the peppers, onions and okra briefly and add to the gumbo. Add the bay leaf, thyme, and spices, and cook a further 30 minutes over gentle heat. Remove the bay leaf, adjust the seasoning and serve.

Crab Meat Balls

Preparation Time: 40-50 minutes **Cooking Time:** 3 minutes per batch of six
Serves: 6-8

Delicious as a first course or a cocktail snack, crab meat balls can be made ahead, then coated and fried at the last minute.

Ingredients

1lb fresh or frozen crab meat, chopped finely
4 slices white bread, crusts removed and made into crumbs
1 tbsp butter or margarine
1 tbsp flour
½ cup milk
½ red or green chili, seeded and finely chopped

1 green onion, finely chopped
1 tbsp chopped parsley
Salt
Flour
2 eggs, beaten
Dry breadcrumbs
Oil for frying

Combine the crab meat with the fresh breadcrumbs and set aside. Melt the butter and add the flour off the heat. Stir in the milk and return to moderate heat. Bring to the boil, stirring constantly. Stir the white sauce into the crab meat and breadcrumbs, adding the chilli, onion and parsley. Season with salt to taste, cover and allow to cool completely. Shape the cold mixture into 1 inch balls with floured hands. Coat with beaten egg using a fork to turn balls in the mixture or use a pastry brush to coat with egg. Coat with dry breadcrumbs. Fry in oil in a deep sauté pan, saucepan or deep-fat fryer at 350°F until golden brown and crisp – about 3 minutes per batch of 6. Turn occasionally while frying. Drain on paper towels and sprinkle lightly with salt.

New Orleans' distinctive streetcars have a charm all their own.

Creole Eggplant

Preparation Time: 30 minutes **Cooking Time:** about 35 minutes **Serves:** 4

Stuffed eggplants are perfect for a first course or a light meal. Shrimp are the customary filling, but other ingredients substitute well.

Ingredients

2 eggplants
$^2/_3$ cup butter or margarine
1 onion, finely chopped
1 stick celery, finely chopped
1 small red pepper, seeded
    and chopped

1 clove garlic, crushed
Salt and pepper
1 cup cooked, peeled shrimp
Dry breadcrumbs

Cut the eggplants in half lengthwise and remove the stems. Score the cut surface lightly and sprinkle with salt. Leave the eggplants to stand on paper towels for 30 minutes. Rinse, pat dry and wrap in foil. Bake for 15 minutes in a preheated 350°F oven.

Scoop out the center of the baked eggplants, leaving a margin of ¼ inch flesh inside the skins to form a shell. Chop the scooped out flesh roughly. Melt the butter and add the chopped eggplant, onion, celery, pepper and garlic. Cook slowly to soften the vegetables. Season with salt and pepper and add the shrimp. Spoon the mixture into the shells, sprinkle with breadcrumbs and bake in an ovenproof dish for an additional 20 minutes. Serve hot.

The strange shape of the cypress tree adds a mysterious air to the bayou.

Red Bean and Red Pepper Soup

Preparation Time: about 25 minutes **Cooking Time:** about 3 hours **Serves:** 8-10

Red beans are very popular in southern Louisiana, and combined with red peppers and red wine they make a hearty soup.

Ingredients

1lb dried red kidney beans
Water to cover
2 onions, coarsely chopped
3 sticks celery, coarsely chopped
2 bay leaves
Salt and pepper

3 large red peppers, seeded and
    finely chopped
4 tbsps red wine
1-2 cups chicken stock
Lemon wedges and 4 chopped
    hard-cooked eggs to garnish

Soak the beans in the water overnight. Alternatively, bring them to the boil and boil rapidly for 2 minutes. Leave to stand for 1 hour. Drain off the liquid and add the onions, celery, bay leaves, salt and pepper, red peppers, red wine and stock. Bring to the boil over high heat, stirring occasionally. Reduce the heat and allow to simmer, partially covered, for about 3 hours, or until the beans are completely tender. Remove the bay leaves and purée the soup in a food processor or blender. Serve garnished with the chopped hard-cooked egg. Serve lemon wedges on the side.

Eating *al fresco* is popular in New Orleans during the humid summer months.

Maque Choux

Preparation Time: about 25 minutes **Cooking Time:** about 10 minutes **Serves:** 6

Sweetcorn is essential to this recipe, but other vegetables can be added, too. In true Cajun style, use what you have to hand.

Ingredients
4 tbsps oil
2 tbsps butter or margarine
2 medium-size onions, peeled and finely chopped
1 clove garlic, crushed
1 medium-size green pepper, seeded and cut into small dice
6 tomatoes, peeled, seeded and diced
8oz fresh corn kernels or frozen corn
1 cup chicken or vegetable stock
Pinch salt
½ tsp cayenne pepper
4 tbsps heavy cream

Heat the oil in a large casserole and add the butter. When foaming, add the onions and garlic and cook, stirring frequently, for about 5 minutes or until both are soft and transparent but not browned. Add the green pepper, tomatoes, corn and stock. Bring to the boil over high heat. Reduce the heat, partially cover the casserole and allow to cook slowly for about 10 minutes, or until the corn is tender. Add the cayenne pepper and salt and stir in the cream. Heat through and serve immediately.

The mighty waters of the Mississippi River carve their way through Louisiana along a 2,300 mile course to the Gulf of Mexico.

Dirty Rice

Preparation Time: about 20 minutes **Cooking Time:** 30-40 minutes **Serves:** 4-6

The name comes from the mixture of finely chopped chicken livers, celery, green pepper and onions that colors the rice.

Ingredients
1 cup long-grain rice
2 cups water
1lb chicken livers
1 stick celery, roughly chopped
1 green pepper, seeded and
    roughly chopped

2 medium onions, roughly chopped
2 tbsps oil
Salt and pepper
Chopped parsley to garnish

Cook the rice in the water with a pinch of salt. When cooked, leave to stand while preparing the liver. Pick over the chicken livers to remove any fat and discolored portions. Place the livers, celery, pepper and onions in a food processor and process to finely chop the ingredients. The mixture will look soupy.

Heat the oil in a large frying pan and add the liver mixture. Cook over moderate heat, stirring gently. Once the mixture has set, turn down the heat to very low, cover the pan and cook about 30-40 minutes, or until rich golden brown in color. Stir in the cooked rice, fluffing up the mixture with a fork. Heat through, season to taste and serve garnished with chopped parsley.

Top: the modern skyline of New Orleans belies its ancient history as the melting pot of cultures such as French, Indian, Acadian, and Spanish.

Cajun Pies

Preparation Time: 30-40 minutes **Cooking Time:** about 20 minutes **Makes:** 8

We've baked this traditional meat pie in individual portions. It's spicy hot, so add cayenne gradually to taste.

Ingredients
Pastry
3 tbsps butter or margarine
2 eggs

4-6 tbsps milk or water
2½-3½ cups all-purpose flour
Pinch sugar and salt

Filling
2 tbsps butter or margarine
½ small onion, finely chopped
½ small green pepper,
   finely chopped
1 stick celery, finely chopped
1 clove garlic, crushed
¾lb ground pork

1 bay leaf, finely crushed
1 tsp cayenne pepper
Pinch salt
2 tbsps flour
1 cup beef stock
1 tbsp tomato paste
1 tsp dried thyme

To prepare the pastry, soften the butter or margarine in a food processor or with an electric mixer until creamy. Beat in the eggs one at a time and add the milk or water. Sift in 2½ cups flour, sugar and salt and mix until blended. If necessary, add the remaining flour gradually until the mixture forms a ball. Wrap well and refrigerate about 30 minutes. Melt the butter or margarine in a large frying pan and cook the onion, pepper, celery, garlic and pork over moderate heat. Break up the meat with a fork as it cooks. Add the bay leaf, cayenne pepper, salt and flour and cook, scraping the bottom of the pan often, until the flour browns. Pour on the stock and stir in the tomato paste and thyme. Bring to the boil and cook, stirring occasionally, until thickened. Chill thoroughly and remove the bay leaf.

Divide the pastry into 8 pieces and roll each out to a circle about ⅛-inch thick. Spread the chilled filling on half of each circle to within ½ inch of the edge. Brush the edge with water. Fold over and seal the edges together firmly. Crimp the edges with a fork.

Heat oil in a deep sauté pan or a deep-fat fryer to about 350°F. Fry 2 or 3 pies at a time for about 2 minutes, holding them under the surface of the oil with a metal spoon to brown evenly. Remove from the oil with a draining spoon and drain on paper towels. Serve immediately.

Shrimp Remoulade

Preparation Time: 25 minutes **Serves:** 4

The shrimp in this dish "cook" in the refrigerator in a marinade that is piquant with mustard, horseradish and wine vinegar.

Ingredients

1½lbs raw unshelled large shrimp
3 tbsps mild mustard
2 tsps horseradish
1 tbsp paprika
1 fresh chili pepper, seeded and
  finely chopped
1 clove garlic, crushed
Salt

½ cup white wine vinegar
1½ cups oil
6 green onions, sliced
2 sticks celery, thinly sliced
2 bay leaves
2 tbsps chopped parsley
Lettuce and lemon wedges

Shell the shrimp, except for the very tail ends. If desired, the shrimp may be completely shelled. Combine the mustard, horseradish, paprika, chili pepper, garlic and salt in a deep bowl. Mix in the vinegar thoroughly. Add the oil in a thin, steady stream while beating constantly with a small whisk. Continue to beat until the sauce is smooth and thick. Add the green onions, celery, bay leaves and chopped parsley. Cover the bowl tightly and leave in the refrigerator for several hours, or overnight.

Two hours before serving, add the shrimp to the marinade and stir to coat them well. Leave in the refrigerator until ready to serve.

To serve, shred the lettuce finely and place on individual serving plates. Arrange the shrimp on top and spoon over some of the marinade to serve, discarding the bay leaves.

New Orleans restaurants serve an exciting array of Cajun and Creole dishes.

Horseradish Pecan Sauce

Preparation Time: about 15 minutes **Makes:** 2½ cups

This creamy, piquant sauce has a variety of uses. The recipe makes a lot, but a sauce this good won't go to waste.

Ingredients
1 cup sour cream or natural yogurt
4 tbsps prepared horseradish
2 tbsps white wine vinegar
1 tbsp Creole-style mustard or other whole grain mustard

Pinch salt, white pepper and sugar
1 cup whipping cream
6 tbsps finely chopped pecans

Combine sour cream or yogurt and horseradish in a small bowl. Add the vinegar, mustard, sugar, salt and pepper, and stir into the sour cream. Do not over-stir. Chill in the refrigerator for at least 2 hours.

Whip the cream until soft peaks form. Mix the chopped pecans into the sour cream sauce and stir in a spoonful of cream to lighten the mixture. Fold in the remaining cream and serve chilled.

Top: New Orleans' French quarter was the original city of the Creoles.

Pecan Chicken

Preparation Time: about 30 minutes **Cooking Time:** 40 minutes **Serving:** 4

Pecans are often used in the South in both sweet and savory dishes. Here, their rich, sweet taste complements a stuffing for chicken.

Ingredients

4 boned chicken breasts
3 tbsps butter or margarine
1 small onion, finely chopped
3oz pork sausage meat
1½ cups fresh breadcrumbs
1 tsp chopped thyme
1 tsp chopped parsley
1 small egg, lightly beaten

1 cup pecan halves
1 cup chicken stock
1 tbsp flour
2 tbsps sherry
Salt and pepper
Chopped parsley or 1 bunch
   watercress to garnish

Cut a small pocket in the thick side of each chicken breast using a small knife. Melt 1 tbsp butter in a small saucepan and add the onion. Cook a few minutes over gentle heat to soften. Add the sausage meat and turn up the heat to brown. Break up the sausage meat with a fork as it cooks. Drain any excess fat and add the breadcrumbs, herbs and a pinch of salt and pepper. Allow to cool slightly and add enough egg to hold the mixture together. Chop pecans, reserving 8, and add to the stuffing. Using a small teaspoon, fill the pocket in each chicken breast with some of the stuffing.

Melt 1 tbsp butter in a casserole and place in the chicken breasts, skin side down first. Brown over moderate heat and turn over. Brown the other side quickly to seal. Pour in the stock, cover the casserole and cook for about 25-30 minutes in a preheated 350°F oven until tender. When chicken is cooked, remove it to a serving plate to keep warm. Reserve cooking liquid.

Melt remaining butter in a small saucepan and stir in the flour. Cook to a pale straw color. Strain on the cooking liquid and add the sherry. Bring to the boil and stir constantly until thickened. Add the pecans and seasoning. Spoon some of the sauce over the chicken. Garnish with chopped parsley or a bouquet of watercress.

Creole Oxtails

Preparation Time: about 30 minutes **Cooking Time:** 3½ hours **Serves:** 8-10

Oxtails are very economical, but rich in flavor. As they cook, they thicken their own sauce, so very little flour is needed.

Ingredients

4½lbs oxtails
Flour for dredging
Salt and pepper
2 onions, coarsely chopped
1 large green pepper, coarsely chopped
3 sticks celery, coarsely chopped
4 cloves garlic, crushed
2lbs canned tomatoes
2 cups beef stock

2 tbsps red wine vinegar
2 tbsps dark brown sugar
Pinch dried thyme
1 bay leaf
Pinch cayenne pepper
Oil for frying
1 tbsp Dijon or Creole mustard
Dash Tabasco
Chopped parsley

Trim excess fat from the oxtails and cut them into 2 inch pieces. Place a few pieces in a sieve and sprinkle over flour, salt and pepper. Shake the sieve to dredge the pieces of meat lightly in flour and repeat until all pieces are coated. Heat the oil in a large casserole or saucepan and brown the meat in several batches. When all the oxtails are browned, remove them to a plate and add the onion, green pepper, celery and garlic to the pan or casserole. Cook over moderately high heat, stirring until the vegetables have softened but not browned. Return the oxtails to the pan and add the tomatoes, stock, vinegar, brown sugar, thyme, bay leaf and cayenne pepper. Bring to the boil and then reduce the heat. Cover and cook gently on top of the stove or in a preheated 350°F oven for about 3½ hours, or until the meat is very tender. When the oxtails are cooked, transfer them to a serving dish and remove the bay leaf from the sauce. Skim the fat and purée the vegetables and the sauce in a food processor until smooth. Add the mustard, dash of Tabasco and a pinch of salt, if necessary. Spoon over the oxtails and sprinkle with chopped parsley, if desired.

Barbecued Shrimp

Preparation Time: about 15 minutes **Cooking Time:** about 5 minutes **Serves:** 2

It's the sauce rather than the cooking method that gives this dish its name. It's spicy, zippy and hot.

Ingredients

1lb large shrimp, cooked and
    unpeeled
½ cup unsalted butter
1 tsp each white, black and
    cayenne pepper
Pinch salt
1 tsp each chopped fresh thyme,
    rosemary and marjoram

1 clove garlic, crushed
1 tsp Worcestershire sauce
½ cup fish stock
4 tbsps dry white wine
Cooked rice

Remove the eyes and the legs from the shrimp. Melt the butter in a large frying pan and add the white pepper, black pepper, cayenne pepper, herbs and garlic. Add the shrimp and toss over heat for a few minutes. Remove the shrimp and set them aside. Add the Worcester sauce, stock and wine to the ingredients in the pan. Bring to the boil and cook for about 3 minutes to reduce. Add salt to taste. Arrange the shrimp on a bed of rice and pour over the sauce to serve.

Fresh crabs, shrimp and crawfish are popular ingredients in Cajun cooking.

Grillades

Preparation Time: 25 minutes **Cooking Time:** 20 minutes **Serves:** 4

Thin slices of beef are quickly fried and then cooked in a rich brown sauce.
Add a dash or two of Tabasco according to taste.

Ingredients

4-8 pieces frying steak, depending
  on size
1 tbsp oil
1 tbsp butter or margarine
1 tbsp flour
6 green onions
1 clove garlic, crushed

1 tsp chopped thyme
2 tsps chopped parsley
3 tomatoes, peeled, seeded
  and chopped
1 cup beef stock
Dash Tabasco
Salt

Place the meat between 2 sheets of plastic wrap or waxed paper and pound
with a rolling pin or a meat mallet to flatten slightly. Heat the oil in a large frying
pan and brown the meat quickly, a few pieces at a time. Set the meat aside.
Melt the butter or margarine in the frying pan and add the flour. Cut the white
part off the green onions and chop it finely. Add to the flour and butter,
reserving the green tops for later use. Add garlic to the pan and cook the
mixture slowly, stirring frequently until it is a dark golden brown. Add the
herbs, tomatoes, stock, Tabasco and salt to taste, and bring to the boil. Cook
about 5 minutes to thicken and add the steaks. Cook to heat the meat
through. Chop the green tops of the onions and sprinkle over the steaks to
garnish.

Top: cargo ships and supertankers are a common sight on the Mississippi.

Veal Jardinère

Preparation Time: 25 minutes **Cooking Time:** 40 minutes **Serves:** 4

Jardin, French for garden, denotes a colorful garnish of vegetables, in this case a selection of carrots, beans, peas and tiny onions.

Ingredients

4 large veal chops	1½ cups beef stock
Oil for frying	6 tbsps white wine
1 tbsp butter or margarine	Salt and pepper
1 carrot, peeled and diced	3oz green beans, topped, tailed
12 button onions	and sliced
1 tbsp flour	2oz peas

Heat about 2 tbsps of the oil in a large frying pan. Trim the chops to remove most of the fat. Fry on both sides in the hot fat until browned. Melt the butter or margarine in a medium saucepan. Peel the onions and add to the butter with the carrot. Cook slowly to soften. Sprinkle on the flour and cook to a good golden brown. Add the stock, wine, salt and pepper and bring to the boil. Cook until thick. Pour the fat from the veal and pour in the sauce. Add the beans and peas and cook until the veal is tender – about 25 minutes.

A street vendor offers refreshment in the French quarter of New Orleans.

Creole Court Bouillon

Preparation Time: 30 minutes **Cooking Time:** 20 minutes **Serves:** 4

Different from a gumbo, this is still a classic Creole soup-stew. Usually, it's prepared with redfish, local to the region, but any firm whitefish will substitute.

Ingredients

Fishbones
1 bay leaf, 1 sprig thyme and
  2 parsley stalks
2 slices onion
1 lemon slice
6 black peppercorns
1½ cups water
6 tbsps oil
6 tbsps flour
1 large green pepper, seeded
  and finely chopped

1 onion, finely chopped
1 stick celery, finely chopped
2lbs canned tomatoes
2 tbsps tomato paste
1 tsp cayenne pepper
Pinch salt and allspice
6 tbsps white wine
2 whole plaice, filleted and skinned
2 tbsps chopped parsley

Place the fishbones in a large stockpot along with the skin from the fish fillets. Add the bay leaf, thyme, parsley, onion, lemon, peppercorns, and water and bring to the boil. Lower the heat and simmer for 20 minutes. Strain and set aside.

Heat the oil and add the flour. Cook slowly, stirring constantly, until golden brown. Add the green pepper, onion and celery, and cook until the flour is a rich dark brown and the vegetables have softened. Strain on the stock and add the canned tomatoes, tomato paste, cayenne pepper, salt and allspice. Bring to the boil and then simmer until thick. Add the wine. Cut the fish fillets into 2 inch pieces and add to the tomato mixture. Cook slowly for about 20 minutes, or until the fish is tender. Gently stir in the parsley, taking care that the fish does not break up. Adjust the seasoning and serve.

Sweet Potato and Sausage Casserole

Preparation Time: about 35 minutes **Cooking Time:** 45 minutes **Serves:** 6

This close relative of the French soufflé is easier to make, and includes two Southern favorites – sweet potato and sausage.

Ingredients

2lbs sweet potatoes
2 tbsps oil
8oz sausage meat
1 small onion, finely chopped
2 sticks celery, finely chopped

½ green pepper, finely chopped
Pinch sage and thyme
Pinch salt and pepper
2 eggs, separated

Peel the sweet potatoes and cut them into 2-inch pieces. Place in boiling water to cover and add a pinch of salt. Cook quickly, uncovered, for about 20 minutes or until the sweet potatoes are tender to the point of a knife. Drain them well and leave them to dry. Purée the potatoes using a potato masher.

While the potatoes are cooking, heat the oil in a large frying pan and add the sausage meat. Cook briskly, breaking up with a fork until the meat is golden brown. Add the onion, celery and green pepper, and cook for a further 5 minutes. Add the sage, thyme and a pinch of seasoning. Beat the egg yolks into the mashed sweet potatoes and, using an electric mixer or a hand whisk, beat the egg whites until stiff but not dry.

Drain any excess fat from the sausage meat and combine it with the sweet potatoes. Fold in the whisked egg whites until thoroughly incorporated. Spoon the mixture into a well-buttered casserole dish or soufflé dish and bake in a preheated 375°F oven until well risen and brown on the top – about 25-30 minutes. Serve immediately.

Blackened Fish

Preparation Time: 20 minutes **Cooking Time:** 2 minutes per side for each fillet
Serves: 4

Cajun cooks all have their own special recipes for the spice mixture, but all agree that the food should have a very brown crust when properly blackened.

Ingredients
4 fish steaks, about 8oz each
1 cup unsalted butter
1 tbsp paprika
1 tsp garlic powder
1 tsp cayenne pepper

½ tsp ground white pepper
1 tsp finely ground black pepper
2 tsps salt
1 tsp dried thyme

Melt the butter and pour about half into each of four custard cups and set aside. Brush each fish steak liberally with the remaining butter on both sides. Mix together the spices and thyme and sprinkle generously on each side of the steaks, patting it on by hand.

Heat a large frying pan and add about 1 tbsp butter per fish steak. When the butter is hot, add the fish. Turn the fish over when the underside is very brown and repeat with the remaining side. Add more butter as necessary during cooking. When the top side of the fish is very dark brown, repeat with the remaining fish steaks, keeping them warm while cooking the rest. Serve the fish immediately with the cups of butter for dipping.

The sedate charm of New Orleans belies its turbulent history.

Chicken Gumbo

Preparation Time: 30 minutes **Cooking Time:** 1 hour 25 minutes **Serves:** 4-6

The African influence on Creole cuisine includes this soup-stew, which takes its name from the African word for okra.

Ingredients

3lb chicken, cut into 6-8 pieces
½ cup oil
1 cup flour
2-3 dried red chili peppers or
   1-2 fresh chili peppers
1 large onion, finely chopped
1 large green pepper, roughly
   chopped
3 sticks celery, finely chopped

2 cloves garlic, crushed
8oz andouille sausage or garlic
   sausage, diced
4 cups chicken stock
1 bay leaf
Dash Tabasco
Salt and pepper
4oz fresh okra
Cooked rice

Heat the oil in a large sauté pan or frying pan and brown the chicken on both sides, 3-4 pieces at a time. Transfer the chicken to a plate and set it aside.

Lower the heat under the pan and add the flour. Cook over a very low heat for about 30 minutes, stirring constantly until the flour turns a rich, dark brown. Take the pan off the heat occasionally, so that the flour does not burn. Add the chili peppers, onion, green pepper, celery, garlic and sausage to the roux and cook for about 5 minutes over very low heat, stirring continuously. Pour on the stock and stir well. Add the bay leaf and a dash of Tabasco, if desired, and return the chicken to the pan. Cover and cook for about 30 minutes or until the chicken is tender.

Top and tail the okra and cut each part into 2-3 pieces. If okra is small, leave whole. Add to the chicken and cook for a further 10-15 minutes. Remove the bay leaf and serve the Gumbo over rice.

Spiced Lamb

Preparation Time: 25 minutes **Cooking Time:** 35 minutes **Serves:** 4

French influence is evident in this dish, but the Creole touch is, too, with a good pinch of allspice and bright red peppers.

Ingredients

1lb lamb neck fillet
1 tsp fresh dill, chopped
1 tsp rosemary, crushed
1 tsp thyme, chopped
2 tsps mustard seeds, crushed
  slightly
2 bay leaves
1 tsp coarsely ground black pepper
½ tsp ground allspice
Juice of 2 lemons

1 cup red wine
2 tbsps oil
2 tbsps butter or margarine
1 small red pepper, seeded and
  sliced
3oz button mushrooms, left whole
3 tbsps flour
½ cup beef stock
Salt

Place the lamb in a shallow dish and sprinkle on the dill, rosemary, thyme and mustard seeds. Add the bay leaves, pepper, allspice, lemon juice and wine, and stir to coat the meat thoroughly with the marinade. Leave for 4 hours in the refrigerator. Heat the oil in a large frying pan and add the red pepper and mushrooms and cook to soften slightly. Remove with a draining spoon.

Reheat the oil in the pan and add the lamb fillet, well drained and patted dry. Reserve marinade. Brown meat quickly on all sides to seal. Remove from the pan and set aside with the vegetables. Melt the butter in the pan, and when foaming, add the flour. Lower the heat and cook the flour slowly until a good, rich brown. Pour in the beef stock and the marinade. Bring to the boil and return the vegetables and lamb to the pan. Cook about 15 minutes, or until the lamb is tender, but still pink inside.

Slice the lamb fillet thinly on the diagonal and arrange on plates. Remove the bay leaves from the sauce and spoon over the meat to serve.

Crawfish Etoufée

Preparation Time: about 20 minutes **Cooking Time:** about 15 minutes **Serves:** 4

This is a thick stew usually made with the local seafood.

Ingredients

$^1/_3$ cup butter or margarine
1 small onion, chopped
1lb crawfish or shrimp
6 tbsps flour
1 cup water or fish stock
1 tbsp tomato paste

2 tbsps chopped parsley
2 tsps chopped dill
Salt and pepper
2 tsps Tabasco or to taste
Cooked rice

Melt half the butter or margarine, add the onion and cook to soften slightly. Add crawfish and cook quickly until it curls. Remove to plate. Add the flour to the pan and cook slowly until golden brown, stirring frequently. Pour on the water and stir vigorously to blend. Add tomato paste and bring to the boil. Add parsley, dill, Tabasco and seasoning to taste and return the onions and the scampi to the sauce. Heat through for 5 minutes and serve over rice.

The bayou winds its way to the Gulf through land settled by the Acadians.

Gingersnap Pork Chops

Preparation Time: about 20 minutes **Cooking Time:** 50 minutes **Serves:** 4

Ginger-flavored cookies give a spicy lift to pork chop gravy, thickening it at the same time.

Ingredients

4 even-sized pork chops, loin
   or shoulder
1 tsp ground black pepper
Pinch salt
1 tsp ground ginger
½ tsp each rubbed sage, cayenne
   pepper, ground coriander and
   paprika

Pinch dried thyme
2 tbsps oil
2 tbsps butter
1 small onion, finely chopped
1 stick celery, finely chopped
½ clove garlic, crushed
1½ cups chicken stock
12-14 gingersnap cookies

Trim the chops if they have excess fat. Mix together the herbs and spices and press the mixture onto the chops firmly on both sides. Heat the oil in a large frying pan and, when hot, add the chops. Brown on both sides and remove to a plate. Add the butter to the frying pan and, when foaming, add the onions, celery and garlic. Cook to soften and pour on the stock. Return the chops to the pan, cover and cook for about 30-40 minutes, or until tender.

When the chops are cooked, remove them to a serving dish and keep them warm. Crush the gingersnaps in a food processor. Alternatively, place the gingersnaps in a plastic bag and use a rolling pin to crush them. Stir the crushed gingersnaps into the pan liquid and bring to the boil. Stir constantly to allow the gingersnaps to soften and thicken the liquid. Boil rapidly for about 3 minutes to reduce, and pour over the chops to serve.

The unspoiled bayou area of southern Louisiana is home to a variety of wildlife.

Chicken with Eggplant and Smoked Ham Stuffing

Preparation Time: about 30 minutes **Cooking Time:** 5-6 minutes **Serves:** 4-6

Eggplants and smoked ham are favorite Cajun ingredients. They add interest to roast chicken in this rich stuffing.

Ingredients

3lb roasting chicken
1 small eggplant
2 tbsps butter or margarine
2 shallots, finely chopped
4oz smoked ham, chopped
1½ cups fresh breadcrumbs
1 tsp chopped fresh thyme

1 tsp chopped fresh oregano
2 tsps chopped parsley
Salt and pepper
Pinch cayenne pepper
1-2 eggs, beaten
2 tbsps additional butter, softened

Cut the eggplant in half lengthwise and remove stem. Lightly score the surface with a sharp knife and sprinkle with salt. Leave to stand for about 30 minutes for the salt to draw out any bitter juices. Melt 2 tbsps butter in a medium saucepan and when foaming, add the shallots. Cook slowly to soften slightly.

Rinse the eggplant and pat dry. Cut into ½ inch cubes. Cook with the shallot until fairly soft. Add the remaining stuffing ingredients, beating in the egg gradually until the mixture just holds together. Add salt and pepper to taste. Remove the fat from just inside the chicken cavity and fill with the stuffing. Tuck the wing tips under the chicken to hold the neck flap down. Stitch up the cavity opening on the chicken or secure with skewers. Tie the legs together and place the chicken in a roasting pan. Spread over the remaining softened butter and roast in a pre-heated 350°F oven for about 1 hour, or until the juices from the chicken run clear when the thickest part of the thigh is pierced with a sharp knife. Leave the chicken to stand for 10 minutes before carving. If desired, make a gravy with the pan juices.

Seafood Pan Roast

Preparation Time: about 40 minutes **Cooking Time:** 30 minutes **Serves:** 4

This mixture of oysters and crab is a descendant of French gratin recipes. It's quick to make and other seafood may be added.

Ingredients

24 small oysters on the half shell
1 cup fish stock
1 cup light cream
$1/3$ cup butter or margarine
6 tbsps flour
1 bunch green onions, chopped
2oz parsley, chopped

2 tbsps Worcestershire sauce
½ tsp Tabasco
Pinch salt
1 large or 2 small cooked crabs
4 slices bread, crusts trimmed and
    made into crumbs

Remove the oysters from their shells with a small, sharp knife. Place the oysters in a saucepan and strain over any oyster liquid. Add the fish stock and cook gently until the oysters curl around the edges. Remove the oysters, keep them warm and strain the liquid into a clean pan. Add the cream to the oyster liquid and bring to the boil. Allow to boil rapidly for about 5 minutes.

Remove crab claws and legs. Turn the crabs over and push out the body with your thumbs. Remove the stomach sac and lungs (dead man's fingers) and discard. Cut the body in four sections with a large, sharp knife and pick out the meat with a skewer. Crack claws and legs to extract the meat. Leave the small legs whole for garnish, if desired. Scrape out the brown meat from inside the shell and combine it with the breadcrumbs and white meat from the body and claws.

Melt the butter or margarine in a medium-size saucepan and stir in the flour. Cook gently for 5 minutes. Add the onions and parsley and cook a further 5 minutes. Pour over the cream and fish stock mixture, stirring constantly. Add the Worcester sauce, Tabasco and salt, and cook about 15-20 minutes over low heat, stirring occasionally. Fold in the crab meat and breadcrumb mixture. Place the oysters in the bottom of a buttered casserole or individual dishes and spoon the crab meat mixture on top. Broil to brown, if desired, and serve immediately.

Chicken and Sausage Jambalaya

Preparation Time: 35-40 minutes **Cooking Time:** 20-25 minutes **Serves:** 4-6

A jambalaya varies according to what the cook has to hand. It could contain seafood, ham, poultry, sausage or a tasty mixture of them all.

Ingredients

3lbs chicken portions, skinned, boned, and cut into cubes
3 tbsps butter or margarine
1 large onion, roughly chopped
3 stick celery, roughly chopped
1 large green pepper, seeded and roughly chopped
1 clove garlic, crushed
1 tsp each cayenne, white and black pepper
1 cup uncooked rice
14oz canned tomatoes
6oz smoked sausage, cut into ½ inch dice
3 cups chicken stock
Salt

Use the chicken bones, skin, onion and celery trimmings to make stock. Cover the ingredients with water, bring to the boil and then simmer slowly for 1 hour. Strain and reserve.

Melt the butter or margarine in a large saucepan and add the onion. Cook slowly to brown and then add the celery, green pepper and garlic and cook briefly. Add the three kinds of pepper and the rice, stirring to mix well. Add the chicken, tomatoes, sausage, stock, and salt, and mix well. Bring to the boil, then reduce the heat to simmering and cook about 20-25 minutes, stirring occasionally until the chicken is done and the rice is tender. The rice should have absorbed most of the liquid by the time it has cooked.

Steamboats have plied the Mississippi for over 200 years, although today it is mainly tourists that they carry.

Crepes a l'Orange

Preparation Time: 30 minutes **Cooking Time:** 45 minutes **Serves:** 4-6

This dish is an American cousin of Crepes Suzette. It's easier than it seems, because it can be prepared in advance and reheated to serve.

Ingredients

1 cup all-purpose flour	½ cup sugar
1 tbsp oil	Grated rind of 1 orange
1 whole egg	4 tbsps finely chopped pecans
1 egg yolk	½ cup orange juice mixed with
1 cup milk	2 tsps cornstarch
Oil for frying	4 oranges, peeled and segmented
1lb cream cheese or low fat	4 tbsps orange liqueur
soft cheese	

Sift the flour into a mixing bowl and make a well in the center. Pour the oil, whole egg and egg yolk into the center of the well and beat with a wooden spoon. Gradually beat in the milk, incorporating the flour slowly. Set aside for 30 minutes. Beat the cheese and sugar together with the orange rind until light and fluffy. Stir in the chopped pecans and set aside.

Heat a small crepe pan or frying pan and pour in a small amount of oil. Wipe over with a paper towel for a thin coating of oil on the bottom. Pour a small amount of batter (about 2 tbsps) into the hot pan and swirl the batter to coat the base evenly. Pour out the excess to re-use. Cook until the bottom is a light golden brown and turn over. Cook the other side and stack up the crepes on a plate. Repeat with remaining batter to make 12 small or 6 large crepes. Spread some of the filling on the speckled side of each crepe and roll up or fold into triangles. Place in a warm oven while preparing the sauce. Pour orange juice and cornstarch mixture into a saucepan and bring to the boil, stirring constantly. Boil until thickened and clear. Stir in the orange segments and liqueur. Spoon sauce over crepes to serve.

Cherries Jubilee

Preparation Time: 30 minutes **Cooking Time:** 10 minutes **Serves:** 4-6

This makes a special, elegant pudding, but an easy one, too. The contrast of hot brandied cherries and cold ice cream or whipped cream is sensational.

Ingredients

1½lbs black cherries, fresh
   or canned
2-4 tbsps sugar

¾ cup brandy
Vanilla ice cream or
   whipped cream

If using fresh cherries, wash them, remove the stems and pit, if desired, but leave the cherries whole. Combine them with 4 tbsps sugar in a saucepan and cook over gentle heat until the cherries soften and the juices run. If using canned cherries, combine the juice with 2 tbsps sugar and heat through to dissolve the sugar. Pit the cherries, if desired, but leave them whole and add to the juice. Pour the brandy into a separate saucepan or a large ladle. Heat the brandy and ignite with a match. Combine the brandy with the fruit and leave until the flames die down naturally. Spoon the fruit over ice cream or on its own into serving dishes to be topped with whipped cream. Serve immediately.

St.Louis Cathedral in the heart of New Orleans' Vieux Carre (Old Square).

Calas

Preparation Time: 40 minutes **Cooking Time:** 40-45 minutes **Makes:** about 24

These small rice cakes are crisp outside, soft and light inside. They are delicious served hot with coffee or tea.

Ingredients

1½-2 cups long-grain rice, cooked
1 cup all-purpose flour
1 tsp baking powder
Pinch salt
½ cup sugar

2 eggs, separated
6 tbsps milk
Grated rind of 1 lemon
4 tbsps raisins
Powdered sugar

Cook the rice, rinse, drain and leave to cool completely. Sift the flour, baking powder and salt into a mixing bowl and stir in the sugar. Beat the yolks with the milk and add gradually to the dry ingredients, stirring constantly, to make a thick batter. Stir in the rice. Beat the egg whites until stiff but not dry, and fold into the batter along with the lemon rind and raisins.

Lightly oil the base of a heavy frying pan and place over moderate heat. When the pan is hot, drop in about 1 tbsp of batter and if necessary, spread into a small circle with the back of the spoon. Cook until brown on one side and bubbles form on the top surface. Turn over and cook the other side. Cook 4-6 at a time. Repeat until all the batter is used, keeping the cakes warm. Sprinkle with powdered sugar and serve.

New Orleans' French Quarter is famous for its nightlife.

Brown Sugar Cookies

Preparation Time: 20 minutes **Cooking Time:** 10-12 minutes
Makes: about 36 cookies

This rather thick dough bakes to a crisp golden brown cookie, perfect as an accompaniment to ice cream or fruit salad.

Ingredients

1¼ cups packed light brown sugar
3 tbsps light corn syrup
4 tbsps water
1 egg
2⅓ cups all-purpose flour

1 tbsp ground ginger
1 tbsp baking soda
Pinch salt
1 cup finely chopped pecans

Mix the brown sugar, syrup, water and egg together in a large bowl. Beat with an electric mixer until light. Sift flour with the ginger, baking soda and salt into the brown sugar mixture and add the pecans. Stir by hand until thoroughly mixed. Lightly oil three baking sheets and drop the mixture by spoonfuls about 2 inches apart. Bake in a pre-heated 375°F oven until lightly browned around the edges – about 10-12 minutes. Leave on the baking sheet for 1-2 minutes before removing with a palette knife to a wire rack to cool completely.

Music is a crucial part of Cajun and Creole culture and as a consequence musicians can be found playing on street corners all over the state.

Pralines

Preparation Time: 25 minutes **Cooking Time:** 20 minutes **Makes:** 12-16

A sugary, crunchy and thoroughly delectable confection with pecans. These are a favorite treat in the Bayou country and all over the South.

Ingredients
1½ cups unsalted butter
1 cup sugar
1 cup packed light brown sugar
1 cup milk
½ cup heavy cream
1 cup chopped pecans
2 tbsps vanilla or rum extract
1 tbsp water
Butter or oil

Melt the butter in a large, heavy-based pan. Add the sugars, milk and cream and bring mixture to the boil, stirring constantly. Reduce the heat to simmering and cook to a deep golden brown syrup. Stir continuously. After about 20 minutes, drop a small amount of the mixture into ice water. If it forms a hard ball, the syrup is ready. The hard ball stage registers 250°F on a sugar thermometer. Add the pecans, flavoring and water. Stir until the mixture stops foaming. Grease baking sheets with butter or oil and drop on the mixture by spoonfuls into mounds about 2 inches in diameter. The pralines will spread out as they cool. Allow to cool completely before serving.

Sightseeing carriages are the best way to capture the spirit of what was once the city of the Creoles and is now know as New Orleans' French Quarter.

Syrup Cake

Preparation Time: about 20 minutes **Cooking Time:** 45 minutes **Makes:** 1 cake

Rather like gingerbread, but with a spicy taste of cinnamon, nutmeg and cloves, this cake can be served cool with coffee or tea or warm with cream.

Ingredients

1 cup vegetable shortening	1 tsp cinnamon
1 cup molasses	¼ tsp ground nutmeg
3 eggs, beaten	Pinch ground cloves
3 cups all-purpose flour	4 tbsps chopped pecans
1 tbsp baking powder	4 tbsps raisins
Pinch salt	

Cream the shortening until light and fluffy. Add the molasses and beat with an electric mixer. Add the eggs one at a time, beating well in between each addition. Sift the flour together with a pinch of salt and baking powder. Combine with the molasses mixture and add the spices. Stir in the nuts and raisins and pour the mixture into a lightly greased 9 x 13 inch baking pan. Bake for about 45 minutes in a pre-heated 375°F oven. To test for doneness, insert a skewer into the center of the cake. If it comes out clean, the cake is done. Allow to cool and cut into squares to serve.

Intricate lace balconies lend a romantic air to some of Louisiana's finest buildings.

Appetizers:
 Crab Meat Balls 12
 Creole Eggplant 14
 Gumbo Z'Herbes 10
 Red Bean and Red Pepper Soup 16
Barbecued Shrimp 32
Blackened Fish 42
Brown Sugar Cookies 64
Cajun Pies 22
Calas 62
Cookies and Desserts:
 Brown Sugar Cookies 64
 Calas 62
 Cherries Jubilee 60
 Crepes a l'Orange 58
 Pralines 66
 Syrup Cake 68
Cherries Jubilee 60
Chicken and Sausage Jambalaya 56
Chicken Gumbo 44
Chicken with Eggplant and Smoked Ham
 Stuffing 52
Crab Meat Balls 12
Crawfish Etoufée 48
Creole Court Bouillon 38
Creole Eggplant 14
Creole Oxtails 30
Crepes a l'Orange 58
Dirty Rice 20
Fish and Seafood:
 Barbecued Shrimp 32
 Blackened Fish 42
 Crawfish Etoufée 48
 Creole Court Bouillon 38

 Seafood Pan Roast 54
 Shrimp Remoulade 24
Gingersnap Pork Chops 50
Grillades 34
Gumbo Z'Herbes 10
Horseradish Pecan Sauce 26
Maque Choux 18
Meat Dishes:
 Cajun Pies 22
 Creole Oxtails 30
 Gingersnap Pork Chops 50
 Grillades 34
 Spiced Lamb 46
 Sweet Potato and Sausage
  Casserole 40
 Veal Jardinère 36
Pecan Chicken 28
Poultry:
 Chicken and Sausage Jambalaya 56
 Chicken with Eggplant and Smoked
  Ham Stuffing 52
 Pecan Chicken 28
Pralines 66
Red Bean and Red Pepper Soup 16
Seafood Pan Roast 54
Shrimp Remoulade 24
Side Dishes:
 Dirty Rice 20
 Horseradish Pecan Sauce 26
 Maque Choux 18
Spiced Lamb 46
Sweet Potato and Sausage Casserole 40
Syrup Cake 68
Veal Jardinère 36